Stay-At-Home Delight

Activities for Adults to Nurture
Joy, Calm, Courage & Connection

Copyright © 2020 by Crystal Lee.

All rights reserved. No part of this publication may be reproduced, distributed or transmitted in any form or by any means, including photocopying, recording, or other electronic or mechanical methods, without the prior written permission of the publisher, except in the case of brief quotations embodied in critical reviews and certain other noncommercial uses permitted by copyright law. For permission requests, write to the author, at:

Crystal Lee / Relocal
relocalvancouver@gmail.com

Ordering Information:
Quantity sales. Special discounts are available on quantity purchases by corporations, associations, and others. For details, contact Crystal Lee at relocalvancouver@gmail.com.

Stay-At-Home Delight: Activities for Adults to Nurture Joy, Calm, Courage & Connection / Crystal Lee.
—1st ed.
ISBN 9781777327507

Message from the Author

Phew! What a year 2020 has been. I know it hasn't been easy to stay cooped up at home - surrounded by four walls and separated from loved ones. "Life has been disrupted" is an understatement.

Please know that your staying at home makes a difference to tackling the coronavirus pandemic. As a daughter of elderly and chronically ill parents, thank you for staying home and giving our healthcare teams the resources to support those most in need. Thank you for keeping yourself and others safe.

From my own self isolation in a shared 700-square-foot laneway house, I've had lots of time to think about life, the current state of the world, and what the future might hold. What could I possibly do to create a more hopeful world when I'm saddened by daily news, overwhelmed by work and chores, trying to maintain a healthy relationship in a tight space, and feeling generally blah?

As a public health nerd turned life coach, my answer is in this tiny book: Start by taking small action, right at home.

I hope that the activities in this book will help you feel grounded. I hope you will learn new things about who you are and what you want. I hope you will be inspired to continue moving forward with confidence and meaningful action.

Crystal

P.S. Don't forget you can download and print the colouring pages in this book at https://relocal.ca/delightful-bonus

Introduction

When you think of staying at home, how do you feel? Lonely and distant from your favourite people and places? Bored of familiar activities? Constricted by small spaces?

What if instead you could feel calm in a welcoming environment and joy from simple actions? What if time at home allowed you to revive meaningful projects and connections?

When you are used to working, socializing, and exploring outside of your home, it can feel uncomfortable to stay indoors for an extended period of time. With a little intention and guidance however, that discomfort can be transformed into an opportunity to learn about yourself, develop new skills, and enjoy life.

This book contains stay-at-home activities designed to help you nurture joy, calm, courage, and connection – key ingredients to a happy, healthy life. Though the activities may sound simple, you may still experience resistance. It's normal! Afterall, it's easier to sit on the couch and binge watch shows.

To get going, start with activities that feel easier so you'll have small wins to celebrate. The suggestions in this book are meant to inspire you. You are very welcome to make adjustments as desired. Reflection prompts are sprinkled throughout to help you get the most out of the experience. Go at your own pace and have fun!

SECTION 1: JOY

Potential Obstacles

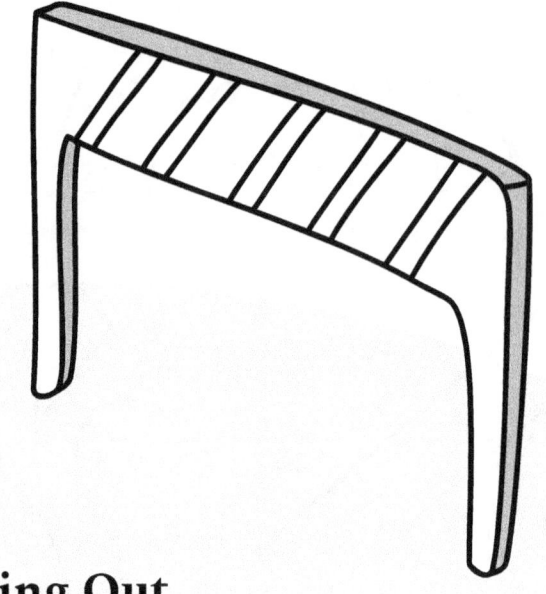

Fear of Missing Out

Do you have trouble slowing down and being alone? Are you always itching to get out because you think that's where all the fun is? STOP. Joy can be found right where you are, just as you are.

Comparison Trap

Your joy will look different from someone else's joy, so stop comparing.

Activities to Nurture Joy

Joy can be sparkly and loud. Joy can also be quiet and special. Joy is yours to experience in this moment and the next. The following activities will help you discover simple ways to tickle your senses and connect with your heart.

Listen to a song which you haven't heard in a long time

Bonus points if you pull out a record, CD, or cassette! What memories do you have of this song? What is the significance?

Watch a critter go about its day

What is it doing? Where do you think it came from and where is it going?

Run your hands through your closet and let your fingers graze each piece of clothing

Which pieces make you want to linger? How come?

Light a candle and watch its flame dance

Notice its colours and movement. How would you describe its energy? What about your energy?

Take 3 big belly breaths. Laugh out each exhale with the ha ha ha sound

How easy or hard is this for you? Notice and keep breathing.

Open a window and watch the world go by for five minutes

When was the last time you simply observed the world?

Bake something and enjoy every bite

Touch it. Smell it. Savour it slowly. On a scale of 1 to 10, how satisfied are you right now?

Fill in Your Own Activities

My Discoveries About Joy

I enjoy
_____
_____
_____

I find it easy to
_____
_____
_____

I smile when
_____
_____
_____

When I slow down, I can appreciate
_____
_____
_____

The next time I have five minutes to do anything I want, I would like to
_____
_____
_____

Other reflections:
_____
_____
_____
_____
_____
_____

SECTION 2: CALM

Potential Obstacles

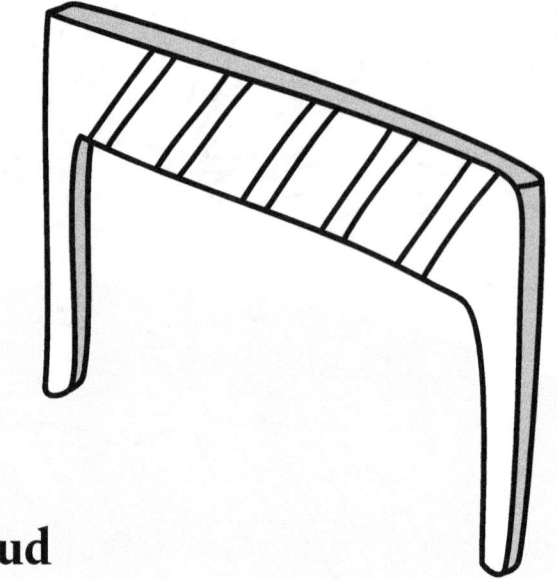

Clutter Cloud

Clutter is a form of organization that doesn't make sense for your brain or physical space. Once you give things a place to belong, things will fall into place with greater ease and calm.

Stuck in Overwhelm

Be kind to yourself. Accept that you are human and can only handle so much. Acknowledge when you feel overwhelmed, then pick one or two things to focus on. Move one day at a time.

Activities to Nurture Calm

Calm is the sensation of steady breaths. It's knowing that things are going to be okay. Calm feels centred and open at the same time, welcoming new possibilities. The following activities will invite spaciousness into your home and mind.

Organize your junk drawer

Empty it and start from scratch. What belongs in that drawer? How could you organize compartments within the whole? Little messes side by side are more manageable than one big mess.

Clear off your dining table or coffee table

Pick up each object on the table and ask yourself: Where could this go? Does it make more sense in the recycling bin, trash, or compost? Guide each item to its next destination. Then start dreaming up beautiful meals and activities that will take place on the newly cleared surface!

Tend to your plants

Pick out brown leaves. Check the moisture of the soil. Empathize with its needs. Give it the sunshine, water, and nutrition needed to thrive.

File away papers

Shred what you don't need and keep what you do. Let go of the things that no longer serve you and keep the things that do.

Mend an article of clothing

Rather than filling the bottom of your closet with neglected items, put your mending skills to use and feel great about putting clothes back into rotation, not the landfill.

Sweep your entryway and make it welcoming

Have you ever considered what it's like to arrive at your home? What do you want guests to feel when they enter? What do YOU want to feel when you enter? Unless you are going for a spooky vibe, it's time to remove the cobwebs and personalize your home with your unique flair.

Walk slowly through your home

Take a step every three seconds. With each step, notice what catches your eye. Keep going until you have walked through every room. What is something that wants your attention in your home?

Fill in Your Own Activities

My Discoveries About Calm

I feel at ease when I
_____
_____
_____

To develop a sense of calm, I need
_____
_____
_____

I am ready to let go of
_____
_____
_____

When I am at home, I want to feel
_____
_____
_____

I look forward to creating space for
_____
_____
_____

Other reflections:
_____
_____
_____
_____
_____
_____

SECTION 3: COURAGE

Potential Obstacles

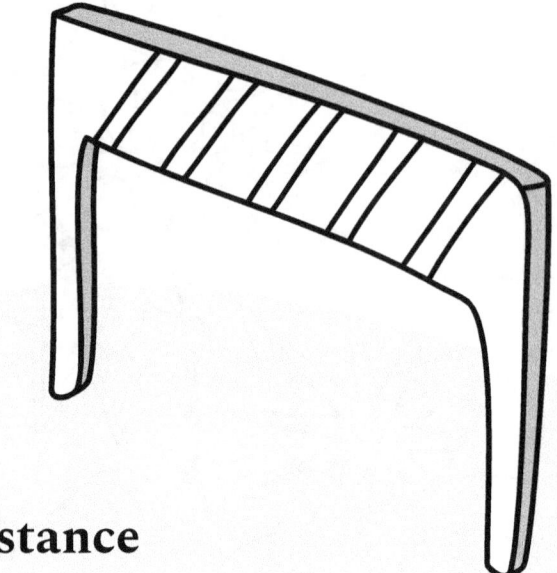

Inner Resistance

Name what you are resistant to, then do it anyway.

Making Something Bigger Than It Is

Do a quick reality check. How much time will it realistically take to complete the task? Break it down into smaller steps. How much time will each step take? Do the steps that you will be able to commit to. When you dedicate pockets of time to a task, you will make progress!

Activities to Nurture Courage

There are likely home activities that you don't want to do even though they will improve your quality of life. Show yourself you can move past your blocks. The following activities will support you in building confidence and courage to overcome inertia.

Clean out the back of your pantry

Pull out every item including those buried in the back. Inspect each and ask: What did you intend to use it for? Let go of whatever attachment you had, and decide now whether you still want to keep it.

Toss out old condiments

Sometimes things go bad. There's no shame in it, but you still need to deal with it. Now is the time to deal with the expired condiments in your fridge! Say goodbye to what's gone bad and allow the compost to transform it into something else.

Try a new recipe

Look up a recipe that will incorporate a neglected ingredient in your kitchen. Trying something new is a great way to practice adaptability, and can result in something delicious too!

Dust hidden corners

Without action, things can settle and fester over time. No more! Grab a vacuum, duster, or old sock, and clear your space of sneezy dust! Notice how much clearer everything looks after taking action?

Sort your wardrobe

Are there pieces that you haven't touched in over a year? That means you have gone through every season and you have not yet circled back to it. Take it as a sign to mend it, upcycle it, or pass it on.

Clean your bathroom

"Yuck!" you might say. But what if it's "Yes!" instead? Say yes to a welcoming space that will greet you each morning and evening, and several times in between. There are few spots in your home which you visit with such regularity. You deserve a fresh space that invites you in.

Maintain laundry traps and pipes

Did you know when you let lint build up in your dryer, it can reduce the efficiency of your machine by 75%? That's a hit to your energy bill and the environment. Can you think of other small actions in your life that would make a big impact?

Fill in Your Own Activities

My Discoveries About Courage

I feel energized from
_____
_____
_____

It feels good to say goodbye to
_____
_____
_____

When I put my heart to it, I know I can
_____
_____
_____

A small action that will help me maintain momentum is
_____
_____
_____

The next time I feel resistance about something, I will remind myself that
_____
_____
_____

Other reflections:
_____
_____
_____
_____
_____

SECTION 4: CONNECTION

Potential Obstacles

Lonely Hearts Club

Being alone doesn't have to feel lonely when you are able to find comfort in solace.

The Oh-So-Boring Life

When life feels dull, it means that you want more. Figure out what you care about and nurture meaningful connections that matter to you.

Terror of Isolation

Remember that you are never truly alone. There are people all around you. Reach out for support if you need it!

Activities to Nurture Connection

Connection can happen even if you are physically alone. It starts with connecting with what is important to you, and turning it outwards. The following activities will connect you with yourself and your community.

Write a letter which you won't send

If you could say anything to anyone, what would you say? To whom? It can be someone you know, someone you don't know, or even your past/present/future self. Let your words flow knowing the words will only ever meet your eyes.

Frame an object that has meaning to you

Whether it's a picture, a quote, or a special doodle, have it in a visible location to remind you of its special place in your heart.

Donate to a cause you care about

If you had a dollar to donate, what cause would you support? Would you consider donating time, resources, or knowledge to further that cause on an ongoing basis? Not only will you meet like-minded people but you'll fill up your heart too!

Support a local business

You are a part of your community, and your community thrives with your support. Is there a local business where you have always received friendly service? Is there a restaurant which you have always wanted to try? Make a purchase from these local businesses and keep your community going strong!

Craft a long email

Pretend it's the early days of email before instant messaging and social media. Write a long email to someone you haven't been in touch with for a while.

Send a postcard

Ask for someone's mailing address and send them good ol' snail mail! Describe the day you had at home just like you would rave about a recent vacation.

Make something and gift it

To share something you created can feel vulnerable, but it's one of the best ways to be truly seen by others. That's the first step to an authentic connection.

Fill in Your Own Activities

My Discoveries About Connection

I cherish
_____
_____
_____

I care deeply about
_____
_____
_____

To bond with others, I can show off my
_____
_____
_____

I would love to meet more people who share my interest in
_____
_____
_____

I feel connected to my community when I
_____
_____
_____

Other reflections:
_____
_____
_____
_____
_____
_____
_____

Over to you!

Now that you have worked through activities to nurture joy, calm, courage, and connection, you are ready to create your next adventure!

What other qualities would you like to nurture?
Examples: creativity, patience, compassion, learning, fitness, simplicity, etc.

What are some activities you can do at home to nurture what you desire?
Use the space below to capture your ideas.

Activities to Nurture

_____
_____
_____
_____
_____
_____
_____
_____

Activities to Nurture

_____
_____
_____
_____
_____
_____
_____
_____

Activities to Nurture

_____
_____
_____
_____
_____
_____
_____
_____

Activities to Nurture

_____
_____
_____
_____
_____
_____
_____
_____

Want ideas? Need support?

Relocal provides empowerment and community to busy people seeking simple and delightful moments in daily life. Past activities have brought people together to make art, explore neighbourhoods, and learn about the natural world. We believe a single special moment can make a person's day, which in turn makes the world a better place.

Visit relocal.ca or follow @relocal.ca on Instagram to learn more!

Acknowledgements

Thank you Vea Coronado for planting a seed for this activity book.
Thank you Marie Schoen for your accountability and editing support.
Thank you Daniel Brard for your ongoing encouragement and feedback.
Thank you Lindsey Smith and Alexandra Franzen for your helpful guidance.

Book design and illustrations by Alex Dewar Design.

About the Author

Crystal Lee is a relocation life & career coach, community builder, and metaphor lover.

Since 2013, she has been helping people clarify their values and purpose to live with greater meaning and joy. Her clients have relocated to new cities, landed dream jobs, started businesses, and successfully navigated major life transitions. Influenced by her laughter yoga training, Crystal's coach approach combines playfulness, discovery, and heart.

As the founder of Relocal, Crystal currently promotes empowerment and community through delightful, do-it-yourself activities and group workshops. She partners with local enthusiasts to deliver experiences that encourage participants to explore their surroundings while developing new knowledge and connections in a relaxed environment. Crystal is passionate about nurturing healthy communities and believes collaboration is key to a happier, healthier, more sustainable world.

Crystal is a Certified Professional Co-Active Coach (CPCC) with a Master of Public Health (MPH) degree from the University of California, Los Angeles. Her undergraduate studies at the University of British Columbia spanned from Cell Biology and Genetics to Asian Studies. To this day, she continues to be fascinated by the natural world and the influence of culture on human behaviours.

In her spare time, you will find Crystal visiting neighbourhood animal friends and tinkering with new writing ideas. Having at one point moved 10 times in 10 years, she is grateful to be living on the unceded territory of the Coast Salish Peoples, also known as Vancouver, Canada.

Connect with Crystal on Instagram @relocal.ca or email relocalvancouver@gmail.com

www.ingramcontent.com/pod-product-compliance
Lightning Source LLC
Chambersburg PA
CBHW081423080526
44589CB00016B/2649